Rose Totino

Pizza Entrepreneur

Rebecca Felix

Checkerboard Library

An Imprint of Abdo Publishing
abdopublishing.com

abdopublishing.com

Published by Abdo Publishing, a division of ABDO, PO Box 398166, Minneapolis, Minnesota 55439. Copyright © 2018 by Abdo Consulting Group, Inc. International copyrights reserved in all countries. No part of this book may be reproduced in any form without written permission from the publisher. Checkerboard Library™ is a trademark and logo of Abdo Publishing.

Printed in the United States of America, North Mankato, Minnesota
102017
012018

THIS BOOK CONTAINS
RECYCLED MATERIALS

Design: Sarah DeYoung, Mighty Media, Inc.
Production: Mighty Media, Inc.
Editor: Liz Salzmann
Cover Photographs: Getty Images; Mighty Media, Inc.
Interior Photographs: Courtesy of Totino's and General Mills Archives, pp. 5, 11, 13, 15, 17, 19, 23, 27, 28 (top), 29 (top, bottom); iStockphoto, p. 9; Minnesota Historical Society, pp. 25, 28 (bottom)
Background Pattern: Shutterstock, cover, pp. 3, 5, 7, 9, 11, 13, 15, 17, 19, 23, 25, 27, 31

Publisher's Cataloging-in-Publication Data
Names: Felix, Rebecca, author.
Title: Rose Totino: pizza entrepreneur / by Rebecca Felix.
Other titles: Pizza entrepreneur
Description: Minneapolis, Minnesota : Abdo Publishing, 2018. | Series: Female foodies |
    Includes online resources and index.
Identifiers: LCCN 2017944045 | ISBN 9781532112690 (lib.bdg.) | ISBN 9781532150418 (ebook)
Subjects: LCSH: Totino, Rose, 1915-1994.--Juvenile literature. | Businesswomen--United States--
    Biography--Juvenile literature. | Pizza industry--Juvenile literature. | Entrepreneurship--Juvenile
    literature.
Classification: DDC 338.76647 [B]--dc23
LC record available at https://lccn.loc.gov/2017944045

Contents

Pizza Pioneer 4

Italian Upbringing 6

Family and Food 8

Baking and Banking 10

Restaurateurs 12

Team Totino 14

Totino's Finer Foods 16

Frozen Pizza Success 18

First Female VP 20

Crisp Crust Success! 22

Beloved Leader 24

Lasting Legacy 26

Timeline 28

Glossary 30

Online Resources 31

Index 32

Chapter 1

Pizza Pioneer

It's Friday night and your best friend is over. You've planned an evening of fun activities and favorite foods. After a bike ride, it's time for dinner. Opening the freezer, you spot the thin red box. Your friend smiles as you pull the Totino's Party Pizza out of its box. In minutes, you'll have a warm, crispy crust topped with perfectly seasoned sauce and tasty cheese!

Rose Totino is the one to thank for your Friday night pizza feast. She began making pizzas in Minnesota in the 1950s. At the time, this Italian dish was new to people in the Midwest. Many had never tried pizza before, or even heard of it!

Totino and her husband Jim opened a pizzeria that became very popular. Then they began making frozen pizzas people baked at home. Totino invented a new kind of dough for these pizzas. It was the first frozen pizza dough that became crispy when baked.

Totino's invention revolutionized the frozen foods world. It greatly improved frozen pizza and was a primary reason

"We didn't plan on setting the world on fire. We just knew how to make good pizza," said Totino of her and Jim's success.

the food became popular in the United States. Today, frozen pizzas are an American **staple**. About 1 million Totino's Party Pizzas are sold every day! The chef behind this successful brand learned to cook in a small Minneapolis, Minnesota, kitchen.

Chapter 2

Chapter 2

Italian Upbringing

Rosenella Winifred Cruciani was born on January 16, 1915, in Minneapolis. Her family called her Rose. Rose was the middle child. She had six brothers and sisters. The Crucianis had **immigrated** to the United States from Italy in 1910. They lived in Pennsylvania for a short time before settling in Northeast Minneapolis.

Northeast Minneapolis was home to many Italian immigrants. The Crucianis and other families in the neighborhood kept their Italian **culture** alive. Rose's mother was a skilled cook who often made classic Italian foods. One was a pie made of dough and topped with sauces, cheese, and sausage. The dish was called pizza and was a family favorite. Rose's mother passed her recipes and cooking talents to her daughter.

The Cruciani family did not have a lot of money. Rose's father taught his children that success came through hard work. At age 16, Rose dropped out of school to work full time and earn money to help her family. Rose cleaned other people's houses. She earned $2.50 each week for this work.

During her childhood, Rose's family had chickens and a garden to help provide food.

Chapter 3

Family and Food

Rose worked very hard at her job. But she made time to socialize too. One night, she attended a party at the Viking Dance Hall in Minneapolis. There, Rose met Jim Totino. Jim was a baker. Like Rose's, his family came from Italy. Also like Rose, Jim had dropped out of school to work.

Rose and Jim began dating. By this time, Rose was working at a local candy factory. In 1934, she married Jim and took his last name. Rose Totino quit her job to take care of her new husband and their home.

Totino and Jim had two daughters, Joanne and Bonnie. Cooking was a large part of Totino's role in caring for her family. She also cooked for others outside her home.

Totino was **involved** in the Parent Teacher Association (PTA) at her daughters' school. She often brought food she made to PTA

Food Bite

Totino also made desserts. One sweet dish she made was a pie topped with cinnamon and sugar.

Rose used dough, cheese, and fresh tomato based sauces to make her pizzas.

meetings. This included homemade pizzas topped with sausage.

People loved Totino's cooking. Many asked her to cook her **delicious** dishes for their events. Soon, Totino began **catering** friends' parties and family gatherings. Many encouraged her to open a restaurant. By the 1950s, Totino and Jim had heard this request enough times that they began to consider it.

Chapter 4

Baking and Banking

The Totinos discussed the idea of opening a restaurant. Totino made several dishes well. But she and Jim felt her pizza was most popular within their community. The couple decided to open a pizzeria.

However, opening a restaurant cost money. The Totinos figured out they would need $1,500 to rent or buy a location, purchase ovens, and more. But the Totinos didn't have this money. So, they asked a bank for a loan.

The Totinos explained their pizzeria idea to bankers. Italian **immigrants** had introduced the United States to pizza in the early 1900s. However, this was mainly in larger cities, such as New York City. Minneapolis was home to fewer Italian immigrants. Because of this, many Minnesotans did not know what pizza was.

The bankers couldn't understand why the Totinos wanted to sell food few people had heard of. But Totino knew people loved her pizza once they tasted it. So, she made a pizza and took it to the bank. The bankers tasted the pizza and granted the Totinos the loan!

Americans were becoming more interested in foreign foods in the 1950s. At this time, pizza was considered exotic to non-Italians!

Chapter 5

Restaurateurs

The Totinos got right to work. They found a location in Northeast Minneapolis, near where they had both been raised. Totino and Jim named their restaurant Totino's Italian Kitchen. The shop opened on February 7, 1951. It was one of the city's first pizzerias.

Totino's Italian Kitchen was a take-out restaurant only. There were no tables for customers to sit at and dine. Instead, people ordered at a counter or window and took pizzas that were hot and ready to eat to go. The Totinos also sold pre-baked pizzas that had cooled. Buyers could take these pizzas home and reheat them.

The pizzeria was immediately successful. On its first day of business, a line of customers stretched for several blocks! From then on during business hours, the shop was always full of people stopping by to pick up pizzas.

Customers loved Totino's pizzeria. But many had the same suggestion for Totino and Jim. These diners told the couple the shop should have tables and chairs so customers could eat at the restaurant.

The original Totino's Italian Kitchen was located near the intersection of Central and Hennepin Avenues.

The Totinos listened. During the shop's early years, the couple added a section of tables and chairs. Totino's Italian Kitchen became a full-service restaurant.

Chapter 6

Team Totino

When Totino's Italian Kitchen first opened, Totino worked there full time. Jim kept his job as a baker for another company. The couple thought this was wise in case the pizzeria didn't earn enough money to support them.

The Totinos needed $85 a month to pay their rent. This meant selling 25 pizzas a week. The Totinos sold this many pizzas and more! Three weeks after the pizzeria opened, Jim quit his job to work there full time.

Totino and Jim made an **efficient** team. Soon, they were making between 400 and 500 pizzas a day! The pizzas were cooked in brick ovens that the couple had specially built for the shop. Totino often handed out free samples to passersby to encourage them to buy pizzas. She also advertised the shop on TV, starring in commercials that aired on local channels.

Business was booming. The Totinos asked family members to work in the restaurant to help keep up. But having help didn't mean the Totinos took a break. The couple often worked at the pizzeria for 18 hours straight!

Jim baked the pizza crusts at Totino's
Italian Kitchen. Totino applied the sauce
and toppings.

Chapter 7

Totino's Finer Foods

After working long shifts at the pizzeria, Totino and Jim were exhausted. Sometimes they were so tired that they wouldn't even count the money they made that day. Instead, they stuffed it into a brown paper bag and went home to sleep.

In the mornings, Totino and Jim paid their **vendors** from the money in the paper bag. These vendors included their bread, milk, and meat suppliers. After paying what they owed, the couple was often surprised at how much money was left.

Over the next ten years, the Totinos saved the restaurant's profits. They eventually had $50,000! They decided to use this money to start a new venture.

Frozen foods were growing in popularity. Totino wanted to make frozen pizzas that customers could buy and then bake at home. These

Food Bite

"Never beyond my wildest dreams did I imagine we'd ever grow this big."
—Rose Totino

At first, Totino's Finer Foods made frozen pasta dinners as well as pizza. However, these products weren't very successful, so the Totinos focused on making pizza.

pizzas could be stored much longer than the pre-baked ones sold at Totino's Italian Kitchen.

In 1962, the Totinos bought an abandoned factory in St. Louis Park, Minnesota. The city is a **suburb** of Minneapolis. There, the frozen-foods company Totino's Finer Foods was born.

Chapter 8

Frozen Pizza Success

The Totinos had made a name for themselves in Minneapolis with their pizzeria. This helped Totino's Finer Foods become a success. Totino's frozen pizzas were first stocked in the city's **supermarkets**. By the mid-1960s, they were being sold around the Midwest.

Although Totino's Finer Foods was doing well, Totino wasn't completely happy with their products. She and Jim were now making hundreds of frozen pizzas in addition to running their restaurant. They made the toppings and sauces for their frozen pizzas. But they did not have the time to make quality dough for the crusts. Instead, they bought pre-made crusts from a supplier in Chicago, Illinois.

Although she was proud of her pizzas overall, Totino did not like their supplier's crust. In fact, she disliked the crust **available** from all suppliers. Totino thought these crusts tasted like cardboard. So, she tried making her own crust for her frozen pizzas.

But Totino ran into the same problems suppliers did. She felt dough made to be frozen and then baked just did not

Totino continued to alter and improve her pizza recipes throughout her lifetime.

retain flavor. It also seemed impossible to make a dough that could be frozen and then become crispy when baked. All frozen pizzas seemed to end up soggy when baked.

Although Totino was still unhappy with the crusts, the company's frozen pizzas became very popular. By the 1970s, Totino's was the top-selling frozen pizza brand in the United States. But Totino's business success didn't end there.

Chapter 9

First Female VP

Totino's Finer Foods hired more and more employees to make its pizzas. In 1971, the Totinos built a new, larger factory for $2.5 million. It was located in Fridley, Minnesota.

By then, Totino's was a well-known brand. Several food manufacturers took notice. One was Minneapolis-based Pillsbury Company. In 1975, it offered to buy the frozen pizza business for $16 million. Totino said she wanted $20 million. Pillsbury didn't want to lose the sale. So, it went above Totino's asking price and offered $22 million!

Totino joined Pillsbury when the company took over Totino's Finer Foods. Totino and her brand were important to Pillsbury. It made Totino the vice president of Pillsbury. She was the first woman to hold this title in the company's more than 100-year history.

As Pillsbury's vice president, Totino traveled the country, giving presentations and earning new customers. She made deals with **supermarkets** to sell her pizzas and other Pillsbury products. She also appeared in Pillsbury ads. Totino thought her new job was very fun!

Rose Totino

By the Numbers

10

number of Totino's pizzas
sold every second
in 2008

56

number of years the
original Totino's Italian
Kitchen location was open

375

number of Totino's Finer Foods
employees in 1975

1993

year Totino became
the first woman in the
Frozen Foods Hall
of Fame

40,000,000

amount in dollars of
annual sales Totino's Finer
Foods had in 1975

300,000,000

approximate number of
Totino's Party Pizzas sold
each year

Chapter 10

Crisp Crust Success!

Totino stayed very busy promoting Pillsbury and selling its products. The Totino's brand was a large part of her focus. Although its frozen pizza continued to sell well under Pillsbury, Totino still wasn't happy with the crust.

When she wasn't traveling or doing promotions, Totino worked at solving the dough problem. Now, she had Pillsbury's team of food scientists to help her! She and the team experimented with new recipes. They also tried new ways of preparing the dough. Finally, they had success.

Totino and the Pillsbury team had been baking the crust before freezing it. Then they tried frying the crust instead of baking it. They were amazed by the results. Frying the crust helped protect it from the process of freezing and then thawing. When it was finally baked, the crust became crispy! It was the first frozen pizza crust of its kind.

Pillsbury introduced Totino's Crisp Crust Pizza in 1978. It was a major **breakthrough**. No other brand selling frozen pizzas at the time had been able to make a crispy crust. Pillsbury patented Totino's dough in 1979.

Introducing the best news since my famous Crisp Crust!

My Microwave Pizza has that delicious Totino's flavor.

Pillsbury

Working To Be Your Preferred Supplier

Totino was portrayed in advertisements as a traditional Italian grandmother. She was often shown in a kitchen wearing a red checked apron.

Chapter 11

Beloved Leader

By 1980, Totino had seen great success in her career at Pillsbury. When she joined the company in 1975, a man named Bill Spoor was head of the company. He gave Totino a five-year contract. However, Spoor promised Totino that she could stay with Pillsbury as long as she wanted to. So, when her contract ended, Totino decided to continue working at the company.

Jim died in 1981. Totino kept herself busy at work after he passed. Many people enjoyed working with her. Totino was known to have a great sense of humor. She also had strong business instincts. She believed that if you train people well and trust them to do a good job, they usually will. Totino's employees said she was great at hiring them and then standing back to let them do their jobs.

Food Bite

The Pillsbury building where Totino worked was just blocks away from Totino's Italian Kitchen.

While working at Pillsbury, Totino appeared in interviews and on talk shows to promote her pizzas.

Totino was still working at Pillsbury in 1985, when she turned 70. This is the age at which Pillsbury required its employees to retire. However, Totino continued to visit the offices regularly after retiring. She stayed **involved** with the company for the rest of her life.

Chapter 12

Lasting Legacy

Totino's pizzas had made her a household name, and a millionaire. She and Jim were always generous. They **donated** millions of dollars to charities and schools. One was Grace High School in Fridley. In 1980, it changed its name to Totino-Grace High School in honor of the couple.

In 1987, Totino sold Totino's Italian Kitchen to her grandson, Steve Elwell. Totino remained **involved** in her brand and restaurant until the end of her life. She died of **cancer** on June 21, 1994.

In 2001, Pillsbury **merged** with food corporation General Mills. Totino's pizzas, now called Party Pizzas, remained a top seller. Totino's name is also on the company's Pizza Rolls. These snacks are not based on a Totino recipe. But they are just as beloved as her famous pizzas.

In 2007, Elwell sold the Totino's Italian Kitchen building to a **developer**. Elwell reopened the restaurant in Mounds View, Minnesota. However, it was not successful in the new location. The restaurant closed for good in 2011.

Totino had a well-known saying. It was, "Be the best and be generous."

Totino's pizza dough revolutionized the frozen foods industry. The **legacy** of her accomplishments lives on through the brand that bears her name. The next time you bite into the crispy crust of a fresh-baked frozen pizza, think of Totino!

Timeline

1915

Rosenella Winifred Cruciani is born on January 16 in Minneapolis, Minnesota.

1934

Rose marries Jim Totino and takes his last name.

1971

Totino's Finer Foods moves into a new, larger factory in Fridley, Minnesota.

1975

Pillsbury buys Totino's Finer Foods for $22 million. Totino becomes Pillsbury's first female vice president.

1985

Totino retires from Pillsbury but remains involved with the company.

1951

Totino's Italian Kitchen opens on February 7 in Northeast Minneapolis.

1962

The Totinos start Totino's Finer Foods and sell frozen pizzas.

1978

Totino's Crisp Crust Pizza is introduced.

1994

Totino dies of cancer on June 21.

2001

Pillsbury merges with General Mills food corporation. Totino's remains a top seller.

Glossary

available – able to be had or used.

breakthrough – an important discovery that happens after trying for a long time to understand or do something.

cancer– any of a group of often deadly diseases marked by harmful changes in the normal growth of cells. Cancer can spread and destroy healthy tissues and organs.

cater – to provide food.

culture – the customs, arts, and tools of a nation or a people at a certain time.

delicious – very pleasing to taste or smell.

developer – a person or company that builds and sells houses or other buildings on a piece of land.

donate – to give.

efficient – able to produce a desired result, especially without wasting time or energy.

immigrate – to enter another country to live. A person who immigrates is called an immigrant.

involve – to take part in something.

legacy – something important or meaningful handed down from previous generations or from the past.

merge – to combine or blend, such as when two or more companies combine into one business.

staple – something used, needed, or enjoyed constantly, usually by many people.

suburb – a town, village, or community just outside a city.

supermarket – a large store that sells foods and household items.

vendor – a person who sells something.

Online Resources

Booklinks
NONFICTION
NETWORK
FREE! ONLINE NONFICTION RESOURCES

To learn more about Rose Totino, visit **abdobooklinks.com**. These links are routinely monitored and updated to provide the most current information available.

Index

A
advertising, 14, 20

B
bankers, 10
birth, 6

C
catering, 9
childhood, 6

D
death, 26

E
education, 6
Elwell, Steve (grandson), 26

F
family, 4, 6, 8, 9, 10, 12, 14, 16, 18, 24, 26
frozen pizza, 4, 5, 16, 17, 18, 20, 22, 27

G
General Mills, 26

H
housecleaning, 6

I
Illinois, 18
immigrants, 6, 10
ingredients, 4, 6, 9, 18
Italian food, 4, 6, 8, 9
Italy, 4, 6

M
marketing, 20, 22
Minnesota, 4, 5, 6, 8, 10, 12, 17, 20, 26

N
New York, 10

P
Parent Teacher Association (PTA), 8
Pennsylvania, 6
Pillsbury Company, 20, 22, 24, 25
pizza crust, 4, 18, 19, 22, 27
pizzeria, 4, 10, 12, 13, 14, 16, 17, 18, 26

R
retirement, 25

S
Spoor, Bill, 24
supermarkets, 18, 20

T
Totino, Bonnie (daughter), 8
Totino, Jim (husband), 4, 8, 9, 10, 12, 14, 16, 18, 24, 26
Totino, Joanne (daughter), 8
Totino-Grace High School, 26
Totino's Crisp Crust Pizza, 22
Totino's Finer Foods, 17, 18, 20
Totino's Italian Kitchen, 12, 13, 14, 16, 17, 18, 26
Totino's Party Pizza, 4, 5, 26
Totino's Pizza Rolls, 26

V
vice president, 20, 24
Viking Dance Hall, 8